Marks and Spencer p.l.c.
Baker Street, London, W1U 8EP

www.marksandspencer.com

Copyright © Exclusive Editions 2002

ISBN: 1-84273-731-7

Printed in China

Produced by the Bridgewater Book Company Ltd.

Photographer Calvey Taylor-Haw

Home Economist Michaela Haw

NOTES FOR THE READER

- This book uses both metric and imperial measurements. Follow the same units of measurement throughout; do not mix metric and imperial.

- All spoon measurements are level: teaspoons are assumed to be 5 ml, and tablespoons are assumed to be 15 ml.

- Unless otherwise stated, milk is assumed to be full fat, eggs and individual vegetables such as carrots are medium, and pepper is freshly ground black pepper.

- Recipes using raw eggs should be avoided by infants, the elderly, pregnant women, convalescents, and anyone suffering from an illness.

- The times given are an approximate guide only. Preparation times differ according to the techniques used by different people and the cooking times may also vary from those given. Optional ingredients, variations or serving suggestions have not been included in the calculations.

contents

introduction   4

smoothies   6

juices & slushes   28

milkshakes   50

drinks for entertaining   72

index   96

introduction

What better way to use the variety of exciting fruits available today than by whipping them up into a delicious smoothie? Juices have also experienced a revival in popularity recently, and are a wonderful way of extracting the nutrients of vegetables and fruits.

Try to have a supply of frozen fruit to hand, such as bananas, strawberries and peaches. To freeze bananas, peel and slice them, then freeze the slices in a single layer on a tray before transferring them to freezer bags. You can do the same with small chunks or slices of other fruits. Always have a supply of ice on hand, too.

An electric juicer is not essential, but if you own one you can enjoy nutritious juices in their natural state. To give you an idea of how much you will need in the way of 'raw materials', 500 g/1 lb 2 oz of apples yield about 225 ml/8 fl oz of juice; the same weight of blackberries yields 325 ml/11 fl oz. For vegetable juices, 500 g/1 lb 2 oz of carrots yield about 225 ml/8 fl oz; the same weight of tomatoes yields 325 ml/11 fl oz.

A food processor or blender will take a lot of the work out of preparing these drinks, and will ensure that they are mixed to the right consistency. Finally, don't forget to have a good selection of glasses and straws ready!

guide to recipe key		
	very easy	Recipes are graded as follows: 1 pea = easy; 2 peas = very easy; 3 peas = extremely easy.
	serves 2	Recipes generally serve two people. Simply halve the ingredients to serve one, taking care not to mix metric and imperial measurements.
	10 minutes	Preparation time. Where chilling or cooling are involved, these times have been added on separately: eg, 15 minutes + 30 minutes to chill.
	10 minutes	Cooking time.

pineapple tango
page 16

summer fruit slush
page 44

smooth nectarine shake
page 56

iced citrus tea
page 82

smoothies

Smoothies are a delicious way to enjoy fruit all year round. Whenever you have a surplus of fruit, instead of reaching for jam recipes, why not set some aside for drinks? Simply prepare and freeze them in the usual way (see page 4), and you will have a constant supply of frozen fruit ready to use for drinks at any time of the year. This is an ideal way to enjoy fruits, even when they are out of season.

forest fruit smoothie

		ingredients	
	extremely easy	350 ml/12 fl oz orange juice	DECORATION
		1 banana, sliced and frozen	slices of fresh strawberry
	serves 2	(see page 4)	
		450 g/1 lb frozen forest fruits	
		(such as blueberries, raspberries	
	10 minutes	and blackberries)	
	—		

Pour the orange juice into a food processor. Add the banana and half of the forest fruits and process until smooth.

Add the remaining forest fruits and process until smooth. Pour the mixture into tall glasses and decorate the rims with slices of fresh strawberry. Add straws and serve.

blueberry dazzler

		ingredients	
	extremely easy	175 ml/6 fl oz apple juice	DECORATION
		125 ml/4 fl oz natural yogurt	whole fresh blueberries
	serves 2	1 banana, sliced and frozen (see page 4)	
	10 minutes	175 g/6 oz frozen blueberries	
	—		

Pour the apple juice into a food processor. Add the yogurt and process until smooth.

Add the banana and half of the blueberries and process well, then add the remaining blueberries and process until smooth. Pour the mixture into tall glasses and add straws. Decorate with whole fresh blueberries and serve.

coconut cream

		ingredients	
	very easy	350 ml/12 fl oz pineapple juice	DECORATION
		90 ml/3¼ fl oz coconut milk	2 tbsp grated fresh coconut
	serves 2	150 g/5½ oz vanilla ice cream	
		140 g/5 oz frozen pineapple chunks	TO SERVE
	15 minutes		2 scooped-out coconut shells, optional
	—		

Pour the pineapple juice and coconut milk into a food processor. Add the ice cream and process until smooth.

Add the pineapple chunks and process until smooth. Pour the mixture into scooped-out coconut shells, or tall glasses, and decorate with grated fresh coconut. Add straws and serve.

melon refresher

		ingredients	
extremely easy		250 ml/9 fl oz natural yogurt	DECORATION
		100 g/3½ oz galia melon, cut into chunks	wedges of melon
serves 2		100 g/3½ oz cantaloupe melon, cut into chunks	
15 minutes		100 g/3½ oz watermelon, cut into chunks	
—		6 ice cubes	

Pour the yogurt into a food processor. Add the galia melon chunks and process until smooth.

Add the cantaloupe and watermelon chunks along with the ice cubes and process until smooth. Pour the mixture into glasses and decorate with wedges of melon. Serve at once.

pineapple tango

		ingredients	
	extremely easy	125 ml/4 fl oz pineapple juice	DECORATION
		juice of 1 lemon	wedges of fresh pineapple
	serves 2	100 ml/3½ fl oz water	
		3 tbsp brown sugar	
		175 ml/6 fl oz natural yogurt	
	15 minutes	1 peach, cut into chunks and frozen	
		100 g/3½ oz frozen pineapple chunks	
	—		

Pour the pineapple juice, lemon juice and water into a food processor. Add the sugar and yogurt and process until blended.

Add the peach and pineapple chunks and process until smooth. Pour the mixture into glasses and decorate the rims with wedges of fresh pineapple. Serve at once.

spiced apple smoothie

		ingredients	
extremely easy		250 ml/9 fl oz apple juice	DECORATION
		½ tsp powdered cinnamon	slices of fresh banana on
serves 2		2 tsp grated fresh root ginger	cocktail sticks
		2 bananas, sliced and frozen (see page 4)	
15 minutes			
—			

Pour the apple juice into a food processor. Add the cinnamon and ginger and process gently until combined.

Add the banana and process until smooth. Pour the mixture into tall glasses and decorate with slices of fresh banana on cocktail sticks. Serve immediately.

breakfast smoothie

		ingredients	
extremely easy		250 ml/9 fl oz orange juice	DECORATION
		125 ml/4 fl oz natural yogurt	slices of fresh banana
serves 2		2 eggs	
		2 bananas, sliced and frozen (see page 4)	
10 minutes			
—			

Pour the orange juice and yogurt into a food processor and process gently until combined.

Add the eggs and frozen bananas and process until smooth. Pour the mixture into glasses and decorate the rims with slices of fresh banana. Add straws and serve.

orange & strawberry cream

		ingredients	
	extremely easy	125 ml/4 fl oz natural yogurt	DECORATION
		175 ml/6 fl oz strawberry yogurt	slices of orange
	serves 2	175 ml/6 fl oz orange juice	whole fresh strawberries
		175 g/6 oz frozen strawberries	
		1 banana, sliced and frozen	
	15 minutes	(see page 4)	
	—		

Pour the natural and strawberry yogurts into a food processor and process gently. Add the orange juice and process until combined.

Add the strawberries and banana and process until smooth. Pour the mixture into tall glasses and decorate with slices of orange and whole strawberries. Add straws and serve.

vegan tropical smoothie

		ingredients	
extremely easy		100 ml/3½ fl oz coconut milk 200 ml/7 fl oz soya milk 100 ml/3½ fl oz pineapple juice 1 tbsp brown sugar 1 ripe mango, stoned and diced 2 tbsp grated fresh coconut 140 g/5 oz frozen pineapple chunks 1 banana, sliced and frozen (see page 4)	DECORATION grated fresh coconut wedges of fresh pineapple
serves 2			
15 minutes			
—			

Put the coconut milk, soya milk, pineapple juice and sugar into a food processor and process gently until combined. Add the mango chunks to the food processor along with the grated coconut and process well.

Add the pineapple chunks and banana and process until smooth. Pour the mixture into glasses, scatter over some grated fresh coconut and decorate the rims with wedges of fresh pineapple. Serve at once.

fig & maple melter

		ingredients	
extremely easy		350 ml/12 fl oz hazelnut yogurt	DECORATION
		2 tbsp freshly squeezed orange juice	toasted chopped hazelnuts
serves 2		4 tbsp maple syrup	
		8 large fresh figs, chopped	
15 minutes		6 ice cubes	
—			

Pour the yogurt, orange juice and maple syrup into a food processor and process gently until combined.

Add the figs and ice cubes and process until smooth. Pour the mixture into glasses and scatter over some toasted chopped hazelnuts. Serve at once.

juices & slushes

Fruit and vegetable juices provide an instant supply of nutritional goodness: their life-giving benefits go straight into the body. The recipes in this chapter offer some exciting ideas, and after you have tried them, why not go on to experiment with your own combinations? The slushes, too, which you will find at the end of this chapter, are great revivers. They are especially refreshing on hot summer days.

tomato blazer

		ingredients	

	extremely easy	500 ml/18 fl oz tomato juice
		dash of Worcestershire sauce
		1 small red chilli, deseeded and
		   chopped
		1 spring onion, trimmed and chopped
		6 ice cubes
			GARNISH
			2 long, thin red chillies, cut into
			   flowers (see below)

	serves 2		
	15 minutes + 30 minutes to chill		
	—		

To make the chilli flowers, use a sharp knife to make six cuts along each chilli. Place the point of the knife about 1 cm/½ inch from the stalk end and cut towards the tip. Put the chillies in a bowl of iced water and leave them for 25–30 minutes, until they have spread out into flower shapes.

Put the tomato juice and Worcestershire sauce into a food processor and process gently until combined. Add the chopped chilli, spring onion and ice cubes and process until smooth.

Pour the mixture into glasses and garnish with the chilli flowers. Add straws and serve.

vegetable cocktail

		ingredients	
	very easy	125 ml/4 fl oz carrot juice	GARNISH
		500 g/1 lb 2 oz tomatoes, skinned,	2 celery sticks
	serves 2	deseeded and roughly chopped	
		1 tbsp lemon juice	
		4 celery sticks, trimmed and sliced	
		4 spring onions, trimmed and roughly	
	15 minutes	chopped	
		25 g/1 oz fresh parsley	
		25 g/1 oz fresh mint	
	—		

Put the carrot juice, tomatoes and lemon juice into a food processor and process gently until combined.

Add the sliced celery along with the spring onions, parsley and mint and process until smooth. Pour the mixture into glasses and garnish with celery sticks. Serve at once.

carrot & red pepper booster

		ingredients
	extremely easy	250 ml/9 fl oz carrot juice
		250 ml/9 fl oz tomato juice
	serves 2	2 large red peppers, deseeded and roughly chopped
		1 tbsp lemon juice
	15 minutes	freshly ground black pepper
	—	

Pour the carrot juice and tomato juice into a food processor and process gently until combined.

Add the red peppers and lemon juice. Season with plenty of freshly ground black pepper and process until smooth. Pour the mixture into tall glasses, add straws and serve.

curried vegetable juice

very easy	
serves 2	
15 minutes	
—	

ingredients

250 ml/9 fl oz carrot juice
4 tomatoes, skinned, deseeded and
  roughly chopped
1 tbsp lemon juice
2 celery sticks, trimmed and sliced
1 cos lettuce
1 garlic clove, chopped

25 g/1 oz fresh parsley
1 tsp curry powder
6 ice cubes
125 ml/4 fl oz water

GARNISH
celery sticks

Put the carrot juice, tomatoes, lemon juice and celery into a food processor and process gently until combined.

Separate the lettuce leaves, then wash them and add them to the food processor along with the garlic, parsley, curry powder and ice cubes. Process until well combined, then pour in the water and process until smooth.

Pour the mixture into tall glasses and garnish with celery sticks. Serve at once.

carrot & ginger energiser

		ingredients	
	very easy	250 ml/9 fl oz carrot juice 4 tomatoes, skinned, deseeded and roughly chopped 1 tbsp lemon juice 25 g/1 oz fresh parsley	1 tbsp grated fresh root ginger 6 ice cubes 125 ml/4 fl oz water GARNISH chopped fresh parsley
	serves 2		
	15 minutes		
	—		

Put the carrot juice, tomatoes and lemon juice into a food processor and process gently until combined.

Add the parsley to the food processor along with the ginger and ice cubes. Process until well combined, then pour in the water and process until smooth.

Pour the mixture into tall glasses and garnish with chopped fresh parsley. Serve at once.

watercress & carrot juice

		ingredients	
	extremely easy	500 ml/18 fl oz carrot juice	GARNISH
		25 g/1 oz watercress	sprigs of fresh watercress
	serves 2	1 tbsp lemon juice	
	10 minutes + 1 hour to chill		
	—		

Pour the carrot juice into a food processor. Add the watercress and lemon juice and process until smooth. Transfer to a jug, cover with clingfilm and chill in the refrigerator for at least 1 hour, or until required.

When the mixture is thoroughly chilled, pour into glasses and garnish with sprigs of fresh watercress. Serve at once.

cranberry sunrise

		ingredients	
extremely easy		300 ml/10 fl oz cranberry juice	DECORATION
		100 ml/3½ fl oz orange juice	slices and spirals of fresh lemon or
serves 2		150 g/5½ oz fresh raspberries	orange
		1 tbsp lemon juice	
10 minutes			
—			

Pour the cranberry juice and orange juice into a food processor and process gently until combined. Add the raspberries and lemon juice and process until smooth.

Pour the mixture into glasses and decorate with slices and spirals of fresh lemon or orange. Serve at once.

summer fruit slush

		ingredients	
	extremely easy	4 tbsp orange juice	DECORATION
		1 tbsp lime juice	fresh whole raspberries and
	serves 2	100 ml/3½ fl oz sparkling water	blackberries on cocktail sticks
		350 g/12 oz frozen summer fruits	
		(such as blueberries, raspberries,	
		blackberries and strawberries)	
	10 minutes	4 ice cubes	
	—		

Pour the orange juice, lime juice and sparkling water into a food processor and process gently until combined.

Add the summer fruits and ice cubes and process until a slushy consistency has been reached.

Pour the mixture into glasses, decorate with whole raspberries and blackberries on cocktail sticks and serve.

iced coffee & chocolate crush

		ingredients	
	extremely easy	400 ml/14 fl oz milk	DECORATION
		200 ml/7 fl oz coffee syrup	grated chocolate
	serves 2	100 ml/3 ½ fl oz peppermint syrup	sprigs of fresh mint
		1 tbsp chopped fresh mint leaves	
		4 ice cubes	
	15 minutes		
	—		

Pour the milk, coffee syrup and peppermint syrup into a food processor and process gently until combined.

Add the mint and ice cubes and process until a slushy consistency has been reached.

Pour the mixture into glasses. Scatter over the grated chocolate, decorate with sprigs of fresh mint and serve.

melon & pineapple slush

		ingredients	
extremely easy		100 ml/3½ fl oz pineapple juice	DECORATION
		4 tbsp orange juice	slices of galia melon
serves 2		125 g/4 oz galia melon, cut into chunks	slices of orange
		140 g/5 oz frozen pineapple chunks	
10 minutes		4 ice cubes	
—			

Pour the pineapple juice and orange juice into a food processor and process gently until combined.

Add the melon, pineapple chunks and ice cubes and process until a slushy consistency has been reached.

Pour the mixture into glasses and decorate with slices of melon and orange. Serve at once.

milkshakes

The milkshake has never lost its popularity. In fact, it seems to be more popular than ever. Milkshakes come in a wide variety of flavours and can be thick or not so thick, depending on the ratio of solid ingredients to milk. For example, many of them contain ice cream, and you can experiment with the thickness by varying the ratio of ice cream to liquid. You can also ring the changes by using a different flavour of ice cream, or by substituting one type of fruit for another.

spiced banana milkshake

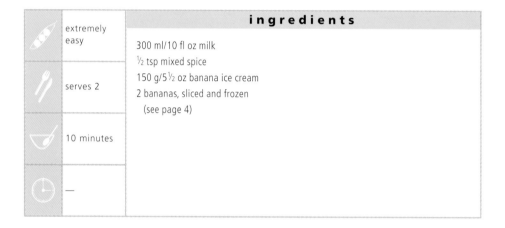

		ingredients
extremely easy		300 ml/10 fl oz milk
		1/2 tsp mixed spice
serves 2		150 g/5 1/2 oz banana ice cream
		2 bananas, sliced and frozen (see page 4)
10 minutes		
—		

Pour the milk into a food processor and add the mixed spice. Add half of the banana ice cream and process gently until combined, then add the remaining ice cream and process until well blended.

When the mixture is well combined, add the bananas and process until smooth. Pour the mixture into tall glasses, add straws and serve at once.

coffee banana cooler

		ingredients
extremely easy		300 ml/10 fl oz milk
		4 tbsp instant coffee powder
serves 2		150 g/5½ oz vanilla ice cream
		2 bananas, sliced and frozen (see page 4)
10 minutes		
—		

Pour the milk into a food processor, add the coffee powder and process gently until combined. Add half of the vanilla ice cream and process gently, then add the remaining ice cream and process until well combined.

When the mixture is thoroughly blended, add the bananas and process until smooth. Pour the mixture into glasses and serve.

smooth nectarine shake

		ingredients
	extremely easy	250 ml/9 fl oz milk
		350 g/12 oz lemon sorbet
	serves 2	1 ripe mango, stoned and diced
		2 ripe nectarines, stoned and diced
	15 minutes	
	—	

Pour the milk into a food processor, add half of the lemon sorbet and process gently until combined. Add the remaining sorbet and process until smooth.

When the mixture is thoroughly blended, gradually add the mango and nectarines and process until smooth. Pour the mixture into glasses, add straws and serve.

tropical storm

		ingredients	
 	very easy	250 ml/9 fl oz milk 50 ml/2 fl oz coconut milk 150 g/5½ oz vanilla ice cream 2 bananas, sliced and frozen (see page 4)	DECORATION grated fresh coconut wedges of fresh pineapple
	serves 2		
	15 minutes	200 g/7 oz canned pineapple chunks, drained 1 pawpaw, deseeded and diced	
	—		

Pour the milk and coconut milk into a food processor and process gently until combined. Add half of the ice cream and process gently, then add the remaining ice cream and process until smooth.

Add the bananas and process well, then add the pineapple chunks and pawpaw and process until smooth. Pour the mixture into tall glasses, scatter over the grated coconut and decorate the rims with pineapple wedges. Serve at once.

peach blush

	very easy	
	serves 2	
	20 minutes	
	—	

ingredients

175 ml/6 fl oz milk
225 g/8 oz canned peach slices,
    drained
2 fresh apricots, chopped
400 g/14 oz fresh strawberries, hulled
    and sliced
2 bananas, sliced and frozen
    (see page 4)

DECORATION
fresh strawberries

Pour the milk into a food processor. Add the peach slices and process gently until combined. Add the apricots and process gently until combined.

Add the strawberries and banana slices and process until smooth. Pour the mixture into glasses and decorate the rims with fresh strawberries. Serve at once.

peach & orange milkshake

		ingredients	
extremely easy		100 ml/3½ fl oz milk	DECORATION
		125 ml/4 fl oz peach yogurt	strips of orange peel
serves 2		100 ml/3½ fl oz orange juice	
		225 g/8 oz canned peach slices, drained	
15 minutes		6 ice cubes	
—			

Pour the milk, yogurt and orange juice into a food processor and process gently until combined.

Add the peach slices and ice cubes and process until smooth. Pour the mixture into glasses and decorate with strips of orange peel. Add straws and serve.

chocolate milkshake

extremely easy	
serves 2	
10 minutes	
—	

ingredients

150 ml/5 fl oz milk
2 tbsp chocolate syrup
400 g/14 oz chocolate ice cream

DECORATION
grated chocolate

Pour the milk and chocolate syrup into a food processor and process gently until combined.

Add the chocolate ice cream and process until smooth. Pour the mixture into tall glasses and scatter over the grated chocolate. Serve at once.

creamy maple shake

extremely easy	
serves 2	
15 minutes	
—	

ingredients

150 ml/5 fl oz milk
2 tbsp maple syrup
400 g/14 oz vanilla ice cream
1 tbsp almond essence

DECORATION
chopped almonds

Pour the milk and maple syrup into a food processor and process gently until combined.

Add the ice cream and almond essence and process until smooth. Pour the mixture into glasses and scatter over the chopped nuts. Add straws and serve.

peppermint refresher

extremely easy	
serves 2	
10 minutes	
—	

ingredients

150 ml/5 fl oz milk
2 tbsp peppermint syrup
400 g/14 oz peppermint ice cream

DECORATION
sprigs of fresh mint

Pour the milk and peppermint syrup into a food processor and process gently until combined.

Add the peppermint ice cream and process until smooth. Pour the mixture into tall glasses and decorate with sprigs of fresh mint. Add straws and serve.

kiwi & lime shake

		ingredients	
extremely easy		150 ml/5 fl oz milk	DECORATION
		juice of 2 limes	slices of kiwi fruit
serves 2		2 kiwi fruit, chopped	strips of lime peel
		1 tbsp sugar	
15 minutes		400 g/14 oz vanilla ice cream	
—			

Pour the milk and lime juice into a food processor and process gently until combined.

Add the kiwi fruit and sugar and process gently, then add the ice cream and process until smooth. Pour the mixture into glasses and decorate with slices of kiwi fruit and strips of lime peel. Serve at once.

drinks for entertaining

The drinks in this chapter present a mouthwatering array of ingredients and flavours, from the stunning Mocha Cream – a feast of coffee, cream and chocolate – to the delicately perfumed Lassi. These drinks will tantalise every palate, yet the good news is that they are alcohol-free, so everyone can enjoy them. You can make them as decorative as you like: suggestions for decoration have been given here, but feel free to experiment with your own.

mocha cream

extremely easy	
serves 2	
15 minutes	
—	

ingredients

200 ml/7 fl oz milk
50 ml/2 fl oz single cream
1 tbsp brown sugar
2 tbsp cocoa powder
1 tbsp coffee syrup or instant
 coffee powder
6 ice cubes

DECORATION
whipped cream
grated chocolate

Put the milk, cream and sugar into a food processor and process gently until combined.

Add the cocoa powder and coffee syrup or powder and process well, then add the ice cubes and process until smooth.

Pour the mixture into glasses. Top with whipped cream, scatter over the grated chocolate and serve.

iced coffee with cream

		ingredients	
very easy		400 ml/14 fl oz water	DECORATION
		2 tbsp instant coffee granules	single cream
serves 2		2 tbsp brown sugar	whole coffee beans
		6 ice cubes	
15 minutes + 1¼ hours to cool			
—			

Use the water and coffee granules to brew some hot coffee, then leave to cool to room temperature. Transfer to a jug, cover with clingfilm and chill in the refrigerator for at least 45 minutes.

When the coffee has chilled, pour it into a food processor. Add the sugar, and process until well combined. Add the ice cubes and process until smooth.

Pour the mixture into glasses. Float single cream on the top, decorate with whole coffee beans and serve.

coffee hazelnut soda

extremely easy	
serves 2	
15 minutes + 1¼ hours to cool	
—	

ingredients

250 ml/9 fl oz water
3 tbsp instant coffee granules
125 ml/4 fl oz sparkling water
1 tbsp hazelnut syrup
2 tbsp brown sugar
6 ice cubes

DECORATION
slices of lime
slices of lemon

Use the water and coffee granules to brew some hot coffee, then leave to cool to room temperature. Transfer to a jug, cover with clingfilm and chill in the refrigerator for at least 45 minutes.

When the coffee has chilled, pour it into a food processor. Add the sparkling water, hazelnut syrup and sugar, and process well. Add the ice cubes and process until smooth.

Pour the mixture into glasses, decorate the rims with slices of fresh lime and lemon and serve.

spiced lemon tea

		ingredients	
extremely easy		400 ml/14 fl oz water	DECORATION
		4 cloves	slices of lemon
serves 2		1 small stick of cinnamon	
		2 tea bags	
		3–4 tbsp lemon juice	
8–10 minutes		1–2 tbsp brown sugar	
3–4 minutes			

Put the water, cloves and cinnamon into a saucepan and bring to the boil. Remove from the heat and add the tea bags. Leave to infuse for 5 minutes, then remove the tea bags.

Stir in lemon juice and sugar to taste. Return the pan to the heat and warm through gently.

Remove the pan from the heat and strain the tea into heatproof glasses. Decorate with slices of lemon and serve.

iced citrus tea

very easy	
serves 2	
15 minutes + 1¼ hours to cool	
3–4 minutes	

ingredients

300 ml/10 fl oz water
2 tea bags
100 ml/3½ fl oz orange juice
4 tbsp lime juice
1–2 tbsp brown sugar
8 ice cubes

DECORATION
wedge of lime
granulated sugar
slices of orange, lemon or lime

Pour the water into a saucepan and bring to the boil. Remove from the heat, add the tea bags and leave to infuse for 5 minutes. Remove the tea bags and leave the tea to cool to room temperature (about 30 minutes). Transfer to a jug, cover with clingfilm and chill in the refrigerator for at least 45 minutes.

When the tea has chilled, pour in the orange juice and lime juice. Add sugar to taste.

Take two glasses and rub the rims with a wedge of lime, then dip them in granulated sugar to frost. Put the ice cubes into the glasses and pour over the tea. Decorate the rims with slices of fresh orange, lemon or lime and serve.

lassi

		ingredients	
	very easy	100 ml/3 ½ fl oz natural yogurt	DECORATION
		500 ml/18 fl oz milk	edible rose petals, optional
	serves 2	1 tbsp rose water	
		3 tbsp honey	
		1 ripe mango, stoned and diced	
	15 minutes	6 ice cubes	
	—		

Pour the yogurt and milk into a food processor and process gently until combined.

Add the rose water and honey and process until thoroughly blended, then add the mango along with the ice cubes and process until smooth. Pour the mixture into glasses, decorate with edible rose petals, if using, and serve.

home-made lemonade

		ingredients	
very easy		150 ml/5 fl oz water	TO SERVE
		6 tbsp sugar	sparkling water
serves 2		1 tsp grated lemon rind	
		125 ml/4 fl oz lemon juice	DECORATION
		6 ice cubes	wedge of lemon
15 minutes + 2½ hours to cool			granulated sugar
			slices of lemon
8–10 minutes			

Put the water, sugar and grated lemon rind into a small saucepan and bring to the boil, stirring constantly. Continue to boil, stirring, for 5 minutes.

Remove from the heat and leave to cool to room temperature. Stir in the lemon juice, then transfer to a jug, cover with clingfilm and chill in the refrigerator for at least 2 hours.

When the lemonade has almost finished chilling, take two glasses and rub the rims with a wedge of lemon, then dip them in granulated sugar to frost. Put the ice cubes into the glasses.

Remove the lemon syrup from the refrigerator, pour it over the ice and top up with sparkling water. The ratio should be one part lemon syrup to three parts sparkling water. Stir well to mix, decorate with slices of fresh lemon and serve.

cherry soda

		ingredients	
	extremely easy	8 ice cubes, crushed 2 tbsp cherry syrup 500 ml/18 fl oz sparkling water	DECORATION maraschino cherries on cocktail sticks
	serves 2		
	5 minutes		
	—		

Divide the crushed ice between two glasses and pour over the cherry syrup.

Top up each glass with sparkling water. Decorate with the maraschino cherries on cocktail sticks and serve.

pineapple float

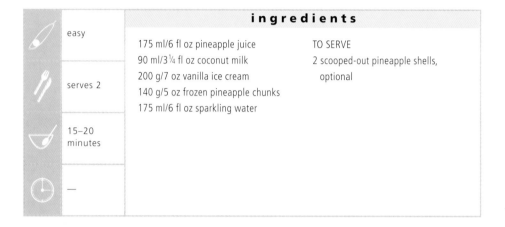

	ingredients	
easy	175 ml/6 fl oz pineapple juice	TO SERVE
	90 ml/3¼ fl oz coconut milk	2 scooped-out pineapple shells,
serves 2	200 g/7 oz vanilla ice cream	optional
	140 g/5 oz frozen pineapple chunks	
15–20 minutes	175 ml/6 fl oz sparkling water	
—		

Pour the pineapple juice and coconut milk into a food processor. Add the ice cream and process until smooth.

Add the pineapple chunks and process well. Pour the mixture into scooped-out pineapple shells or tall glasses, until two-thirds full. Top up with sparkling water, add straws and serve.

raspberry & apple quencher

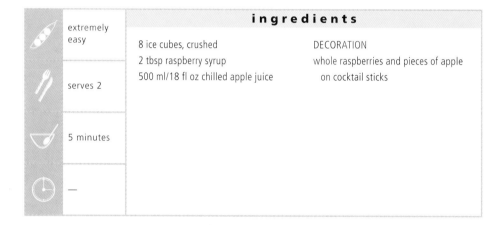

extremely easy	
serves 2	
5 minutes	
—	

ingredients

8 ice cubes, crushed
2 tbsp raspberry syrup
500 ml/18 fl oz chilled apple juice

DECORATION
whole raspberries and pieces of apple
 on cocktail sticks

Divide the crushed ice between two glasses and pour over the raspberry syrup.

Top up each glass with chilled apple juice and stir well. Decorate with the whole raspberries and pieces of apple on cocktail sticks and serve.

carrot & orange cream

extremely easy	
serves 2	
10 minutes	
—	

ingredients

175 ml/6 fl oz carrot juice
175 ml/6 fl oz orange juice
150 g/5½ oz vanilla ice cream
6 ice cubes

DECORATION
slices of orange
strips of orange peel

Pour the carrot juice and orange juice into a food processor and process gently until well combined. Add the ice cream and process until thoroughly blended.

Add the ice and process until smooth. Pour the mixture into glasses, decorate with slices of orange and strips of orange peel and serve.

index

apples
    juice extraction 4
    raspberry & apple quencher 92
    spiced apple smoothie 18

bananas
    breakfast smoothie 20
    coffee banana cooler 54
    frozen 4
    spiced banana milkshake 52
    tropical storm 58
blackberry juice extraction 4
blenders 4
blueberry dazzler 10
breakfast smoothie 20

carrots
    carrot & ginger energiser 38
    carrot & orange cream 94
    carrot & red pepper booster 34
    juice extraction 4
    watercress & carrot juice 40
cherry soda 88
chocolate
    coffee & chocolate crush 46
    milkshake 64
coconut
    coconut cream 12
    tropical storm 58
    vegan tropical smoothie 24
coffee
    coffee & chocolate crush 46
    coffee banana cooler 54
    coffee hazelnut soda 78
    iced coffee with cream 76
    mocha cream 74
cranberry sunrise 42
creamy maple shake 66
curried vegetable juice 36

electric juicers 4
entertaining
    carrot & orange cream 94
    cherry soda 88
    coffee hazelnut soda 78
    home-made lemonade 86
    iced citrus tea 82
    iced coffee with cream 76
    lassi 84
    mocha cream 74
    pineapple float 90
    raspberry & apple quencher 92
    spiced lemon tea 80
fig & maple melter 26

food processors 4
forest fruit smoothie 8

home-made lemonade 86

iced drinks
    citrus tea 82
    coffee & chocolate crush 46
    coffee with cream 76

juices
    carrot & ginger energiser 38
    carrot & red pepper booster 34
    cranberry sunrise 42
    curried vegetable 36
    extraction 4
    tomato blazer 30
    vegetable cocktail 32
    watercress & carrot 40

kiwi & lime shake 70

lassi 84
lemonade 86

melon
    melon & pineapple slush 48
    melon refresher 14
milkshakes
    chocolate 64
    coffee banana cooler 54
    creamy maple 66
    kiwi & lime 70
    peach & orange 62
    peach blush 60
    peppermint refresher 68
    smooth nectarine 56
    spiced banana 52
    tropical storm 58
mocha cream 74

nectarine shake 56

oranges
    carrot & orange cream 94
    orange & strawberry cream 22
    peach & orange milkshake 62

peaches
    frozen 4
    peach & orange milkshake 62
    peach blush 60
peppermint refresher 68

pineapple
    melon & pineapple slush 48
    pineapple float 90
    pineapple tango 16
    tropical storm 58
    vegan tropical smoothie 24

raspberry & apple quencher 92

slushes
    iced coffee & chocolate crush
      46
    melon & pineapple 48
    summer fruit 44
smooth nectarine shake 56
smoothies
    blueberry dazzler 10
    breakfast 20
    coconut cream 12
    fig & maple melter 26
    forest fruit 8
    melon refresher 14
    orange & strawberry cream 22
    pineapple tango 16
    spiced apple 18
    vegan tropical 24
sodas
    cherry 88
    coffee hazelnut 78
spiced drinks
    apple smoothie 18
    banana milkshake 52
    lemon tea 80
strawberries
    frozen 4
    orange & strawberry cream 22
summer fruit slush 44

teas
    iced citrus 82
    spiced lemon 80
tomato blazer 30
tomatoes, juices 4
tropical storm 58

vegan tropical smoothie 24
vegetables
    cocktail 32
    curried vegetable juice 36
    juice extraction 4

watercress & carrot juice 40